Violette, La Petite Araignée Rigolote
Violette, The Witty Little Spider

Written and Illustrated by Thalie Carmigniani

Halo
PUBLISHING
INTERNATIONAL

Halo Publishing International
7550 WIH-10 #800, PMB 2069,
San Antonio, TX 78229

First Edition, May 2024
ISBN: 978-1-63765-608-2
Library of Congress Control Number: 2024909190

Halo Publishing International is a self-publishing company that publishes adult fiction and non-fiction, children's literature, self-help, spiritual, and faith-based books. Do you have a book idea you would like us to consider publishing? Please visit www.halopublishing.com for more information.

Pour ma fille Violette, qui est mon inspiration tous les jours.

Pour mes neveux Luka, Raphaël, et Léo,
et ma nièce Charlotte, que j'aime très fort.

Et pour tous les autres parents et enfants
qui s'embarquent dans le monde bilingue.

For my daughter Violette, who inspires me every day.

For my nephews Luka, Raphaël, and Léo,
and my niece Charlotte, whom I love very much.

And for all the other parents and children who embark on the bilingual journey.

Ce livre appartient à:

This book belongs to:

_____

_____

Je m'appelle Violette.
My name is Violette.

Il était une fois une petite araignée qui s'appelait Violette.
Violette aimait beaucoup monter sur les enfants
parce qu'elle trouvait ça très marrant.

Once upon a time, there was a little spider named Violette.
Violette loved to climb on children because it was so much fun.

Elle commençait par les pieds et vérifiait
qu'il y avait cinq orteils de chaque côté.

She started with the feet and checked that each had five digits.

Coucou!
Good morning!

Elle continuait de marcher jusqu'aux petits genoux,
où elle s'arrêtait pour dire « coucou! ».

She continued her walk all the way up to the knees,
where she waved her hat and said, "Good morning!"

La la la!

Puis elle passait par le bidon et faisait trois petits tours en fredonnant sa chanson.

Then she moved on to the belly and did three little spins while singing a song.

Je t'aime!
I love you!

Sur son chemin, elle se retrouvait souvent
dans le cou et s'amusait à faire plein de bisous.

On her way to the top of the head, she often stopped
at the neck and gave lots of kisses. What a mess!

Ensuite, elle courait vers la tête où elle s'arrêtait pour faire la fête.

Then, she ran to the head and stopped to shake from side to side.

Puis quand elle avait fini, elle redescendait en passant par le nez et marchait jusqu'aux petits pieds.

When she was done, she made her way down by jumping on the nose and running to the toes.

Au revoir!
Bye bye!

Et avant de s'en aller, elle lançait un dernier petit baiser.

And before leaving, she blew one more kiss.

La Fin
The End